This book belongs to

★ ──────────────────────────────── ★

Written by Gaby Goldsack
Illustrated by Michelle White

This is a Parragon Publishing book
This edition published in 2006

Parragon Publishing
Queen Street House
4 Queen Street
Bath BA1 1HE, UK

Copyright © Parragon Books Ltd 2005

Printed in China
ISBN 1-40544-488-6

My Perfect Pony

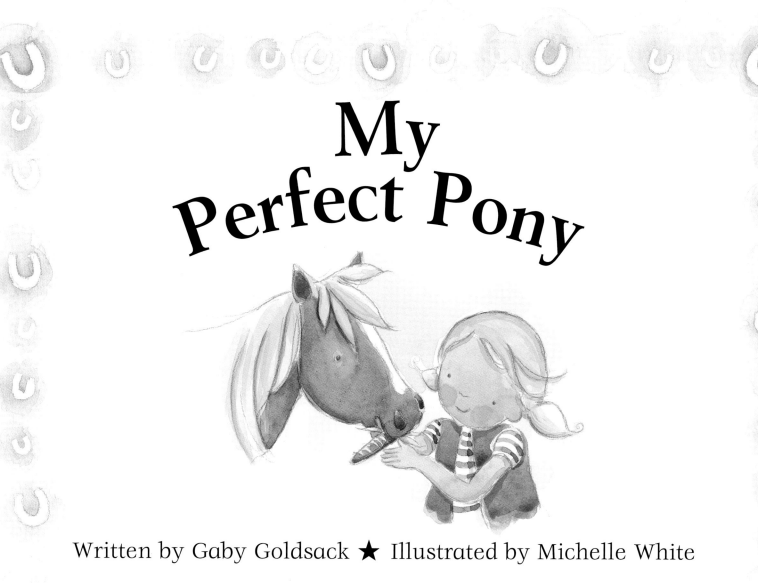

Written by Gaby Goldsack ★ Illustrated by Michelle White

p

It was summertime on Merrymead Farm and all the ponies were grazing in the meadow. They all looked happy, but one little pony looked particularly pleased with the world. His name was Pepper. He was happy because he was the luckiest pony on the whole of Merrymead Farm. He wasn't the most handsome, the smartest, or even the fastest pony, but Pepper didn't mind one bit. He knew he was the luckiest pony on the farm because Lucy—the sweetest, kindest, most loving little girl that a pony could ever wish to meet—owned him.

Lucy adored Pepper. She thought he was perfect in every way.

She gave him a juicy carrot
every time she saw him.

And she spent hours and hours
grooming his unruly mane.

Lucy was never mad or mean, and always took Pepper for the nicest of rides. She ignored the other children and their ponies when they laughed at Pepper for knocking down the odd jump or for going slower than everyone else.

"They're just jealous," she'd whisper, "because you're the best pony on the whole farm." And most of the time, Pepper managed to believe her. After all, Lucy was always right.

One summer evening, Lucy rushed out to the meadow with a piece of paper in her hand.

"Look," she cried. "There's going to be a horse show tomorrow right here on Merrymead Farm! There are going to be games and jumping, and even a showing class. I can't wait. I know that we're going to win lots of lovely ribbons."

Horse Show at Merrymead Farm

Horse Show games
Show jumping
Showing classes

As Lucy rushed off to spread the news, Pepper flicked his ears anxiously. He wasn't sure that he liked the sound of a horse show. It didn't seem like his sort of thing at all. How could he hope to compete against all the other ponies, who were so much bigger, faster, and better-looking than he was?

"Oh dear!" thought Pepper. "Lucy wants lots of lovely ribbons and I don't want to let her down. What am I going to do?"

Later that night, when darkness had fallen over the meadow,
Pepper crept past the other ponies as they slept.
"All I need is a little secret practice," he thought, eyeing up the
jumps at the far end of the meadow. "Then I won't let Lucy down."

Pepper raced toward the jumps at a flat-out gallop.
"Whee," he cried, as he sailed toward the first jump. Then, "Ouch!"
he yelped, as he knocked it with his belly and it fell to the ground.

He barely paused before he bravely raced toward the next jump. But by now he was going way too fast.

There was no way he could take off in time, and he skidded into the jump, knocking the whole thing flying.

As Pepper staggered to his feet,
he heard howls of laughter.
He'd made so much noise that
he'd awakened the other ponies.
"Oh dear!" laughed Bluey, the
largest of the ponies. "I don't
think you're built for jumping."
"Your legs are too short to go fast,"
said Swallow, the quickest pony
on the farm.
"You're far too scruffy for
showing," said Ebony, the sleek
and vain show pony.
"And you're too fat for horse show
games," finished Bonny, who had
won more ribbons than all of
the other ponies.

When all the other ponies had gone back to sleep,
Pepper hung his head in shame and wept.
"They're right," he sniffed. "I'm no good for anything.
I'm bound to let Lucy down. What would she want with a
useless pony like me?"
As these thoughts tumbled through his head, Pepper fell
into a restless, dream-filled sleep.

In his dream, a beautiful white horse appeared
before him. Around her neck hung a shiny, silver charm.
"Don't be afraid," she whispered. "I am the Great White Horse.
I've come to help you." Pepper blinked as she called,

"Fly with me and my lucky charm
to see the best pony on Merrymead Farm."

Then, much to Pepper's surprise, he felt his feet lift from the ground. "Whooaah," he cried, waggling his legs in the air and soaring through the sky. "Hey, I'm flying," he shouted to the Great White Horse. "Now, look below you," said the Great White Horse. Pepper looked down on a familiar scene.

"It's the farm," he cried. "And look, Lucy and I are trotting past the geese."
"Yes, and look at all the other ponies," said the Great White Horse. "While you march bravely past the geese without any fuss, they shake with fear or run away. I bet their owners wish they were more like you."

The Great White Horse reared up and tossed her
flowing mane, and the scene beneath them changed.
"It's the meadow!" smiled Pepper. He watched as Lucy
came out to catch him. As always, he raced up to meet her.
All around, ponies fled in a stampede of hooves. None of
them wanted to be caught by their owners.

Next, Pepper watched as the children got their ponies ready for a ride. He couldn't help smiling as he watched himself and Lucy rubbing noses. That was one of their favorite games. Behind him, Pepper could see Bluey putting back his ears and waving his back leg at his little boy.

"Ooh! That's not nice," gasped Pepper.

"Exactly," said the Great White Horse. "It doesn't matter what happens tomorrow. You are brave, loyal, and kind. You are the perfect pony for Lucy. Just be yourself tomorrow and everything will be all right!"

The following morning Pepper woke up feeling much better. And after Lucy had braided his mane and tail, groomed him until his coat gleamed, and painted his hooves a lovely black color, he felt almost confident. He knew he looked his best. But then, so did all the other ponies.

The first class was the jumping. As Pepper entered the ring, he remembered his failed attempts the night before. But then he remembered the words of the Great White Horse.

"Just be yourself and everything will be all right."

Pepper eyed the jumps, then set off at a steady trot. Slowly but surely, he sailed clear over each jump. "Nearly there," he thought, as he launched himself at the last jump. But, just as he thought he'd made a clear round, his back hoof tapped the pole, and it rattled to the ground. Poor Pepper couldn't believe his bad luck. But Lucy was delighted, particularly when she was given a white ribbon for coming in fourth.

In the egg-and-spoon race, Pepper trotted so steadily that Lucy didn't drop her egg once, unlike many of the other owners whose eggs were flipped this way and that. They didn't win, or even come second, but Lucy was delighted when they were given a yellow ribbon for coming in third.

And they did even better in the pole-bending race, even
though Pepper's round belly made it rather difficult to bend
quickly around the poles.
"Well done," said the judge, as she awarded Pepper a
beautiful red ribbon for coming in second.

The final event of the day was the showing class.

"All the other ponies are much smarter than me," thought Pepper.

But, as he trotted around, he remembered the words of the

Great White Horse.

"Fly with me and my lucky charm

to see the best pony on Merrymead Farm."

He was so busy enjoying himself that it took a few seconds to realize

that the judge was calling to him and Lucy.

"And the winners are Pepper and Lucy," the judge said again as he

pinned a blue ribbon to Pepper's bridle. Then, he hung something

shiny around Lucy's neck.

"It's with great pleasure that I award you the Lucky Charm Award

for best pony in show," he said as he smiled at Lucy.

Pepper looked at the charm and gasped. It was the same as

the one the Great White Horse had worn. Maybe it hadn't

been a dream after all.

"Thank you, Great White Horse," he whispered.

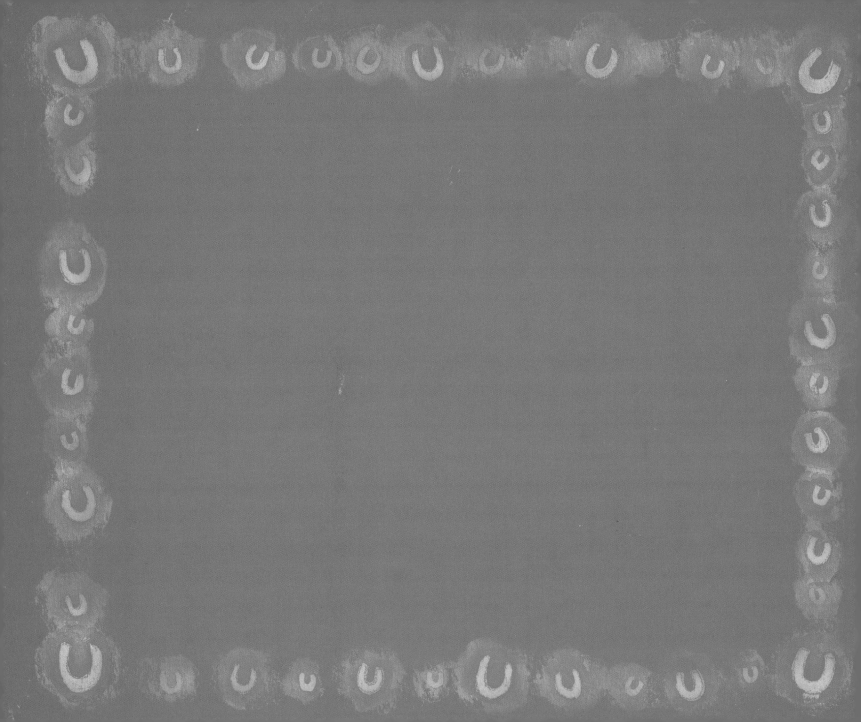